SWU-700-001

BRITISH ARMY UNIFORMS IN 1742

IN THE ART OF JOHN PINE

From "A Representation of the Clothing
of His Majesty's Household and all the Forces upon
the Establishments of Great Britain & Ireland 1742".
Engraved by John Pine,
by order of the Duke of Cumberland.

SOLDIERSHOP PUBLISHING

AUTHOR

John Pine (1690–1756) was a famous English designer, engraver, and cartographer notable for his artistic contribution to the Augustan style and Newtonian scientific paradigm that flourished during the British Enlightenment.

Title: **BRITISH ARMY UNIFORMS IN 1742 - In the art of John Pine**
By Luca Stefano Cristini. Plates of J.Pine First edition September 2016 by Soldiershop.
Cover & Art Design: Luca S. Cristini. ISBN code: 978-88-93271295

Published by Soldiershop publishing, via Padre Davide, 7 - 24050 Zanica (BG) ITALY. www.soldiershop.com

BRITISH ARMY
UNIFORMS IN 1742

*

IN THE ART OF
JOHN PINE

THE XVIII CENTURY UNIFORMS OF THE BRITISH ARMY FROM THE: *"A REPRESENTATION OF THE CLOTHING OF HIS MAJESTY'S HOUSEHOLD AND ALL THE FORCES UPON THE ESTABLISHMENTS OF GREAT BRITAIN & IRELAND 1742".*

This illustrated "war" book was commissioned directly by William Augustus the Duke of Cumberland, the victor of Culloden, to realize a particular gift to his brother, King George II, and shows in 94 colour illustrations the uniform of all units and establishments of the British army in the 1742, some year before Culloden.

It was superbly built by the hands of the great British engraver and artist: John Pine!

Our copy derived from the original preserved at NYPL in the files of Viskuezzen collection.
The book shows 93 of the original 94 plates (92 soldiers in uniforms and a frontispiece).
It show the uniforms and accoutrements of the Household Cavalry and the Horse Cavalry regiments, including the Carabineers and the Dragoons. It also includes the dress of the infantry corps as 1st Foot Guards (Grenadier Guards), the Coldstream Guards and the 3rd Regiment of Foot Guards (Scots Guards). The line regiments are also fully covered, from the Queen's Regiment, the King's Regiment, the Royal Regiment of Fusiliers, and all the other line regiments then established in the British Army.
The last part of the book is devoted to the other corps as ten regiments of Marines, the Regiment of Invalids, the Gentlemen Pensioners and the Yeomen of the Guard. Each plate shows the uniform of the regiment in full, together with (where applicable) horse coverings and the colours of the regiment. each painting has been restored from scratches and usury of time, in order to return the original as it looked like at the time of the original book.
In appendix we have add 10 plates more about works of R.Knotel and other artist, always on British uniform in same year.

This book will be of interest to all historians of the British Army, and uniformology and accoutrements in general.

◀ *William Augustus, Duke of Cumberland, by David Morier (died 1770)*

CONTENTS

*

Preface pag. 5

*

John Pine biography pag. 7

The Duke of Cumberland pag. 8

*

PLATES 1 THE CAVALRY pag. 17
PLATES 2 THE INFANTRY pag. 45
PLATES 3 OTHER CORPS pag. 99
PLATES 4 APPENDIX pag. 113

THE ARTIST

John Pine (1690–1756) was a famous English designer, engraver, and cartographer notable for his artistic contribution to the Augustan style and Newtonian scientific paradigm that flourished during the British Enlightenment.

The Engraver

It is not known where Pine learned his art, although he may have studied under the French artist Bernard Picart (1673–1733), who was associated with a movement described as the *"Radical Enlightenment."* He operated a printshop in London and thus was able to publish books illustrated with his own engravings.

John Pine was probaly as black or of African ancestry. His first important publication, was a group of engravings of the ceremonies attending King George I's establishment of the Order of the Bath (1725).

His other productions include a copy of the Magna Carta, an edition of Horace and a part of one of Virgil, copies of the tapestries celebrating the defeat of the Spanish Armada and hanging in the House of Lords, and the plates of this book ordered by the Duke of Cumberland about the british Army in 1742.

Friendship with Hogarth

Pine was an old friend of William Hogarth, who also began his career as an engraver. It appears likely that their careers were mutually reinforcing, even though Pine remained principally in the field of engraving while Hogarth became a famous painter. Hogarth painted Pine several times; once, in his 1749 engraving The Gate of Calais, depicting him as a fat friar.

Also our image of the artist is a work of Hogarth.

Pine's capacity an valor were recognized in 1743, when he became Engraver of His Majesty's Signet and Seals, and subsequently Bluemantle Pursuivant of Arms in Ordinary. His two son Robeert and Simon, were both painters. Especially Robert Edge Pine (1730–1788), became a notable portrait painter of the late eighteenth century in both England and America. He painted George II and the famous actor David Garrick before emigrating to America where he painted Washington and other figures of the Revolutionary Era.

▲ *John PIne portrait of William Hogath*

▲ William The soldier ... By Arthur Pond

THE APPLICANT

Prince William Augustus, Duke of Cumberland lived from 15 April 1721 to 31 October 1765. was the third and youngest son of George II of Great Britain and Caroline of Ansbach, and Duke of Cumberland from 1726.
This younger son of George II and Queen Caroline, he became a celebrated military leader at a very young age and at twenty five years old commanded the Government forces that defeated the Jacobites at the Battle of Culloden in 1746.

He is often referred to by the nickname given to him by his English Tory opponents: *'Butcher'* Cumberland principally due to his choice after the battle and his oversight of the genocide across the Highlands that followed, but his defeat of the Jacobites also earned him gratitude in the Lowlands and great acclaim in London.

Despite his triumph at Culloden, he had a largely unsuccessful military career. Following the Convention of Klosterzeven in 1757, he never held active military command and switched his attentions to politics and horse racing.

William was born in London in 1721. At the age of four he was created Duke of Cumberland, as well as Marquess of Berkhampstead; Earl of Kennington; Viscount Trematon; and Baron Alderney. He was well educated, and his parents' favourite: his father, George II, would later consider how to make William heir to the throne in preference to his older brother Frederick.

Aged 19, Cumberland joined the Royal Navy, but in 1742 he transferred to the Army, becoming a Major General in December of that year at the age of 21.

In 1743 he saw active service in the middle east, then on 27 June 1743 fought alongside his father at the Battle of Dettingen in Germany during the war of Austrian Succesion (1740-1748). Cumberland was wounded, but considered a hero at home, and promoted to Lieutenant General.

On 11 May 1745, at the age of 24, Cumberland was Commander-in-Chief of the allied British, Hanoverian, Austrian and Dutch troops when he led his troops to a valiant defeat at the Battle of Fontenoy.

CULLODEN AND THE JACOBITE DEFEAT

When Bonnie Prince Charlie marched into England at the head of his Jacobite Army in November 1745, evading Field Marshal Wade's forces to reach Derby, Cumberland was recalled to England to take charge of all forces in Britain. He hotly pursued the Jacobite Army back to the Scottish border, but then returned south to ensure the south coast of England was safeguarded against French attack: leaving the continued pursuit to Lieutenant General Hawley.

But when Hawley was beaten by the Jacobites at the Battle of Falkirk Muir on 17 January 1746, Cumberland headed north, where he arrived in Edinburgh on 30 January.

Now in active pursuit of the Jacobites, Cumberland took time out in Aberdeen to make sure his troops were trained in specific tactics he had developed to withstand the famous highland charge. He set out from Aberdeen towards the main body of the Jacobites at Inverness on 8 April 1746.

By 14 April Cumberland's army had reached Nairn, and the Jacobites marched out from Inverness to meet them at Culloden Moor on 15 April. Instead, Cumberland gave his army the day off to celebrate his 25th birthday. When the two armies did meet on 16 April, the outcome was a decisive victory for Cumberland.

The Duke of Cumberland, however, was interested in doing more than winning a battle. He wanted to ensure that the long series of Jacobite uprisings in Scotland, with previous flare-ups in 1689, 1708, 1715, and 1719, would be brought to an end, once and for all. He was, after all, part of the Hanoverian dynasty the Jacobites were trying to overthrow. A copy of the general orders issued to the Jacobites the day before the battle had been captured on 15 April, and someone, presumably on Cumberland's instruction, had inserted a forged addition, to the effect that no quarter was to be given to any Hanoverian prisoners.

On the morning of the Battle of Culloden, Cumberland's troops were circulated with an order that said: Officers and men will take notice that the public orders of the rebels yesterday was to give us no quarter.

As hints go, it was a heavy one, and in the aftermath of the battle, Cumberland's troops committed widespread atrocities, killing many wounded, surrendering and fleeting Jacobites, as well as bystanders, residents, and just about

▲ *The battle of Culloden of 16 April 1746 by David Morier*

anyone else within reach. Worse was to come. Cumberland established his headquarters at Fort Augustus, which had been named after him during his childhood. From there he sent out columns of troops backed by ships of the Royal Navy to commit what would now be regarded as genocide across the Jacobite areas of the Highlands.

Cumberland actually considered shipping the entire population of these areas to the colonies: but in the end satisfied himself with burning every farmstead, croft and house; with widespread murder and rape; and with rounding up and sending south 20,000 head of cattle, effectively wiping out the entire basis of the economy of the Highlands.

For his activities at Culloden and afterwards, Prince William Augustus came to be known in the Highlands as *"Butcher Cumberland"*.

But in the Lowlands it was a different story. The Glasgow Journal produced a special commemorative edition after Culloden in which they recorded *"the greatest rejoicings that have been known in the city"*.

In May, the General Assembly of the Church of Scotland sent Cumberland a letter noting that it had been able to meet "in a state of peace and security exceeding our greatest hopes... owing to...your generous resolution in coming to be the deliver of this Church and Nation."

Meanwhile, Cumberland was given the freedom of the City of Glasgow, and made Chancellor of both Aberdeen and St Andrews Universities. Most Lowland Scots had little love for the Jacobites, and even less sympathy for those in the Highlands who had become involved in Charles Edward Stuart's destructive adventure.

Back in London, Cumberland was lionised with a special anthem being composed in his honour by Handel: *"See the conqu'ring hero comes."* Despite this, Culloden and its brutal aftermath did begin to take the shine off Cumberland's public image south of the border, and the taunt of *"Butcher Cumberland"* began to take hold.

And it is significant that no British Army regiment ever included Culloden amongst its battle honours. Things got much worse for Cumberland when, in 1757, he was placed in command of British and allied forces defending Hanover from French attack during the Seven Years' War. It was a major humiliation for a dynasty that had its origins and took its name from Hanover that he should fail. George II refused to be bound by Cumberland's agreement to evacuate Hanover, and in disgrace Cumberland resigned from all public office.

After his young nephew George III had succeeded to the throne, Cumberland tried but failed to become Regent. Prince William Augustus, Duke of Cumberland, or if you prefer, *"Butcher Cumberland"*, died in London in 1765, aged just 44.

The British Army in 1742

In the years of the War of the Austrian Succession (1740–1748), of the war in North America and during the Jacobite rising of 1745 in Scotland, executives for the British army were:

1- The War Office, responsible for day-to-day administration of the army, and for the cavalry and infantry.

2- The Board of Ordnance, responsible for the supply of weapons and ammunition, and all needs related the Royal Artillery and Royal Engineers.

3- The Commissariat, responsible for the supply of rations and transport.

In every case the British army was a professional army, well assorted and disciplined – corporal punishment was largely used. Several trooper was not English but German. The officer were mostly of noble classes

On the battlefield and campaign, a commander's staff consisted of an Adjutant General (who handled finance, troop returns and legal matters), and a Quartermaster General (who was responsible for billeting and organising movements). There were separate commanders of the Artillery, and Commissary Officers who handled the supplies. The commander of an Army might also have a Military Secretary, responsible for appointments, courts martial and official correspondence. In the field as in peacetime, the conflicting lines of responsibility often caused problems.

▲ *The March of the Guards to Finchley, is a 1750 oil painting by English artist William Hogarth*

At the beginning of seven years war the name of the first fifty infantry regiment were:

FOOT GUARD

1st Regiment of Foot Guards
2nd Coldstream Regiment of Foot Guards
3rd Scots Regiment of Foot Guards

INFANTRY REGIMENTS

1st Royal
2nd Queen's Royal
3rd Buffs
4th King's Own
5th Bentinck, 1759 Hodgson
6th Guise
7th Royal Fusiliers
8th King's
9th Yorke
10th Pole
11th Bocland
12th Napier
13th Pulteney
14th Jeffries
15th Amherst
16th Handasyd
17th Forbes, 1759 Monckton
18th Royal Irish
19th Lord Beauclerk
20th Kingsley
21st Royal North British Fusileers
22nd Whitmore, 1762 Gage
23rd Royal Welsh Fusiliers
24th Cornwallis
25th Edinburgh
26th Anstruther
27th Inniskilling
28th Bragg, 1759 Townshend
29th Boscawen
30th Earl of Loudoun
31st Holmes
32nd Leighton
33rd Lord Hay
34th Earl of Effingham
35th Otway
36th Lord Robert Manners
37th Stuart
38th Ross, Watson
39th Adlercron
40th Hopson
41st Royal Invalids (Parsons)

42nd Royal Highland (Murray)
43rd Kennedy, 1761 Talbot
44th Abercromby
45th Robinson, 1761 Boscawen
46th Murray
47th Lascelles
48th Dunbar
49th Walsh, Stanwix
50th Abercromby, 1756 Hodgson, 1759 Griffin

Infantry and cavalry units had originally been known by the names of their colonels. This could be confusing every time that the Colonels succeeded each other. In the half of XVIII century a numeral system was adopted, with each regiment gaining a number according to their rank in the order of precedence. In 1739 was formed the first full Scottish regiment, the 42nd Regiment of Foot. For many years, highland regiments were to be the most colourful and distinctive units in the British Army, retaining much of the traditional highland dress such as the kilt. During the 18th century, the battalion was the major tactical unit of the army, and a regiment was a formation of two or more battalions, under a colonel who was a field commander. The function of the Regiment became administrative rather than tactical. The Colonel of a regiment remained an influential figure but rarely commanded any of its battalions in the field. Many regiments consisted of one battalion only, plus a depot and recruiting parties in Britain or Ireland if the unit was serving overseas. Where more troops were required for a war or garrison duties, second, third and even subsequent battalions of a regiment were raised, but it was rare for more than one battalion of a regiment to serve in the same brigade or division.

The infantry regiments were often made up of a single ten-company battalion. The first was a grenadier company. Every battalion was composed from 800 to 1.000 men about. In battle the battalion deployed in three ranks. Every battalion carried two flag, the national flag or King's colors and the regimental flag with the distinctive colour of the regiment.

The cavalry was formed in squadrons. It was divided in: Horse Guard, normal cavalry (Horse) and Dragoons regiments. This superb army was the real pride of the British army. The cavalry of Horse Guards include the Life Guard. Like the use of the time, the British dragoons were created to be used as mounted infantry.

CAVALRY REGIMENTS (IN 1750 ABOUT)

HOUSEHOLD CAVALRY
Life Guards
1st, or His Majesty's Own Troop of Guards
2nd, or The Queen's Troop of Guards
1st Troop, Horse Grenadier Guards
2nd Troop, Horse Grenadier Guards
Royal Horse Guards or The Blues

CAVALRY REGIMENTS

1st (The King's) Regiment of Dragoon Guards
2nd (The Queen's) Regiment of Dragoon Guards
3rd Regiment of Dragoon Guards
1st Regiment of Horse, or The Blue Horse
2nd Regiment of Horse, or The Green Horse
3rd Regiment of Horse (Carabiniers)
4th Regiment of Horse, or The Black Horse

DRAGOONS REGIMENTS

1st (Royal)
2nd (Royal North British)
3rd (King's Own)
4th
5th (Royal Irish)
6th (Inniskilling)
7th (Queen's Own)
8th
9th
10th Mordaunt
11th Ancram
12th Whiteford
13th
14th

ARMY UNIFORMS

The British soldier would have worn the traditional confortable redcoat uniform consisting of the distinctive regimental coat, a white shirt, grey trousers to be held up by a pair of braces, shoes and a cap. The cap may have differed depending on the regiment, but the traditional pattern was the Tricorne. An embroidered "Mitre" was used by the grenadier.

To identify the numerous regiments from one another the colours of the facings on the dress would have differed to reflect the regimental colours. For example, the 34th Regiment of Foot used "pale yellow" facings "lined with a particular trimmed colour line", whilst the 41rd Regiment of Foot used green facings with a "white lining".

There were also stipulations as to the way the men wore their hair. At a time when most of the troops would have had long hair, the regulation was to wear it queued. It was to be "tied a little below the upper part of the collar of the coat, and to be ten inches in length" with one inch of hair below the tie. Soldiers were not allowed to cut their hair as it prevented the queued appearance.

Officers' uniforms were usually in brighter colors, and had different styles. They also had different insignia, and a decorative metal plate over the neck called a gorget.

ARMY MILITARY ENGAGEMENTS IN FIRST HALF OF XVIII CENTURY

- The War of the Spanish Succession (1701–1715) was a major European conflict of the early 18th century.
- War of the Quadruple Alliance (1718–20) - Great Britain, France, Austria and the Dutch Republic versus Italy and Spain
- War of Jenkins' Ear (1739–42) - Great Britain versus Spain
- The Jacobite rebellions were a series of uprisings, rebellions, and wars in Great Britain and Ireland occurring between 1688 and 1746.
- War of the Austrian Succession (1742–48) - Great Britain, Austria and the Dutch Republic versus France and Germany. This War involved most of the powers of Europe over the question of Maria Theresa's succession to the realms of the House of Habsburg. The war included King George's War in North America, the War of Jenkins' Ear, the First Carnatic War in India, the Jacobite rising of 1745 in Scotland, and the First and Second Silesian Wars.

A *Representation* of the CLOATHING of His Majesty's Houshold, and of all the Forces upon the Establishments of GREAT BRITAIN AND IRELAND. 1742.

HONI · SOIT · QUI · MAL · Y · PENSE

PLATES LIST OF ILLUSTRATIONS

Cavarly regiments:

1 1st troop of Horse Grenadier Guards
2 2nd troop of Horse Grenadier Guards
3 Royal north British Dragoons
4 1st troop of Horse Guards
5 2nd troop of Horse Guards
6 3rd troop of Horse Guards
74th troop of Horse Guards
8 Royal Regiment of Horse Guards
9 King's Own Regiment of Horse
10 Queen's Regiment of Horse
11 King's Regiment of Carabiniers
12 4th Regiment of Horse
13 5th Regiment of Horse
14 6th Regiment of Horse
15 8th Regiment of Horse
16 Royal Regiment of Dragoons
17 King's Regiment of Dragoons
18 Royal Irish Regiment of Dragoons
19 4th Regiment of Dragoons
20 6th Regiment of Dragoons
21 8th Regiment of Dragoons
22 9th Regiment of Dragoons
23 10th Regiment of Dragoons
24 11th Regiment of Dragoons
25 12th Regiment of Dragoons
26 13th Regiment of Dragoons
27 14th Regiment of Dragoons

Infantry regiments:

28 King's Regiment of Foot
29 Coldstream Regiment of Guards
30 1st Foot Guard
31 3rd Foot Guard
32 Royal Regiment of Foot
33 Royal EnglishFusiliers
34 Royal Scotch Fusiliers
35 Royal Welsh Fusiliers
36 Royal Regiment of Ireland
37 3rd regiment of Foot
38 5th regiment of Foot
39 6th regiment of Foot
40 8th regiment of Foot
41 9th regiment of Foot
42 10th regiment of Foot
43 11th regiment of Foot
44 12th regiment of Foot
45 13th regiment of Foot
46 14th regiment of Foot
47 15th regiment of Foot

48 16th regiment of Foot
49 17th regiment of Foot
50 19th regiment of Foot
51 20th regiment of Foot
52 22th regiment of Foot
53 24th regiment of Foot
54 25th regiment of Foot
55 26th regiment of Foot
56 27th regiment of Foot
57 28th regiment of Foot
58 29th regiment of Foot
59 30th regiment of Foot
60 31th regiment of Foot
61 32th regiment of Foot
62 33th regiment of Foot
63 34th regiment of Foot
64 35th regiment of Foot
65 36th regiment of Foot
66 37th regiment of Foot
67 38th regiment of Foot
68 39th regiment of Foot
69 40th regiment of Foot
70 41th regiment of Foot
71 42th regiment of Foot
72 43th regiment of Foot
73 44th regiment of Foot
74 45th regiment of Foot
75 46th regiment of Foot
76 47th regiment of Foot
77 48th regiment of Foot
78 49th regiment of Foot
79 50th regiment of Foot

Marine and other corps:

80 His Majesty's Band of Yeomen of the Guard
81 His majesty's Band of Gentleman Pensioners
82 Regiment of Invalid
83 1st Regiment of Marine
84 2nd Regiment of Marine
85 3rd Regiment of Marine
86 4th Regiment of Marine
87 5th Regiment of Marine
88 6th Regiment of Marine
89 7th Regiment of Marine
90 8th Regiment of Marine
91 9th Regiment of Marine
92 10th Regiment of Marine

Appendix:

plates by R.Knotel and other artist

THE COLOUR PLATES

*

1 - THE CAVALRY

1 - 1st troop of Horse Grenadier Guards

2 - 2nd troop of Horse Grenadier Guards

3 - Royal north British dragoons

4 - 1st troop of Horse Guards

5 - 2nd troop of Horse Guards

6 - 3rd troop of Horse Guards

7 - 4th troop of Horse Guards

8 - Royal Regiment of Horse Guards

9 - King's Own regiment of Horse

10 - Queen's Regiment of Horse

11 - *King's Regiment of Carabiniers*

12 - 4th regiment of Horse

13 - 5th regiment of Horse

14 - 6th regiment of Horse

15 - 8th regiment of Horse

16 - Royal Regiment of Dragoons

17 - King's Regiment of Dragoons

18 - Royal Irish Regiment of Dragoons

19 - 4th Regiments of Dragoons

20 - 6th Regiments of Dragoons

21- 8th Regiments of Dragoons

22 - 9th Regiments of Dragoons

23 - 10th Regiments of Dragoons

24 - 11th Regiments of Dragoons

25 - 12th Regiments of Dragoons

26 - 13th Regiments of Dragoons

27 - 14th Regiments of Dragoons

THE
COLOUR
PLATES

*

1 - THE INFANTRY

28 - King's Regiment of Foot

29 - Coldstream Regiment of Guards

30 - 1st Foot Guard

31 - 3rd Foot Guard

32 - Royal Regiment of Foot

33 - Royal English Fusiliers

34 - Royal Scotch Fusiliers

35 - *Royal Welsh Fusiliers*

36 - Royal Regiment of Ireland

37 - 3rd Regiment of Foot

38 - 5th Regiment of Foot

39 - 6th Regiment of Foot

40 - 8th Regiment of Foot

41 - 9th Regiment of Foot

42 - 10th Regiment of Foot

43 - 11th Regiment of Foot

44 - 12th Regiment of Foot

45 - 13th Regiment of Foot

46 - 14th Regiment of Foot

47 - 15th Regiment of Foot

48 - 16 th *Regiment of Foot*

49 - 17th Regiment of Foot

50 - 19th Regiment of Foot

51 - 20th Regiment of Foot

52 - 22th Regiment of Foot

53 - 24th Regiment of Foot

54 - 25th Regiment of Foot

55 - 26th Regiment of Foot

56 - 27th Regiment of Foot

57 - 28th Regiment of Foot

58 - 29th Regiment of Foot

59 - 30th Regiment of Foot

60 - 31th Regiment of Foot

61 - 32th Regiment of Foot

62 - *33th Regiment of Foot*

63 - 34th Regiment of Foot

64 - 35th Regiment of Foot

65 - 36th Regiment of Foot

66 - 37th Regiment of Foot

67 - 38th Regiment of Foot

68 - 39th Regiment of Foot

69 - 40th Regiment of Foot

70 - 41th Regiment of Foot

71 - 42th Regiment of Foot

72 - 43th Regiment of Foot

73 - 44th Regiment of Foot

74 - 45th Regiment of Foot

75 - 46th Regiment of Foot

76 - 47th Regiment of Foot

77 - 48th Regiment of Foot

78 - 49th Regiment of Foot

79 - 50th Regiment of Foot

THE
COLOUR
PLATES

*

2 - OTHER CORPS

80 - His majesty's Band of Yeomen of the Guard

81 - *His majesty's Band of Gentleman Pensioners*

82 - Regiment of Invalid

83 - 1st Regiment of Marine

84- 2nd Regiment of Marine

85 - 3rd Regiment of Marine

86 - 4th Regiment of Marine

87 - 5th Regiment of Marine

88 - 6th Regiment of Marine

89 - 7th Regiment of Marine

90 - 8th Regiment of Marine

91 - 9th Regiment of Marine

92 - 10th Regiment of Marine

THE

COLOUR

PLATES

*

4 - APPENDIX

A - Queen's and King'sRegiment of Dragoons 1742 by R.Knotel

B - Royal North British Dragoons by R.Knotel

C - 6th Horse by R.Knotel

D - Royal Horse Guards by R.Knotel

E - 28th foot (at left) and Royal Scotch Fusiliers by R.Knotel

F - Coldstream Guard Regiment

G . 14th Regiment of Foot

H - King's Regiment of Carabiners

1 - 32th Regiment of Foot

K - 40th Regiment of Foot

SOLDIERS, WEAPONS & UNIFORMS ALREADY PUBLISHED
(SOME TITLES)

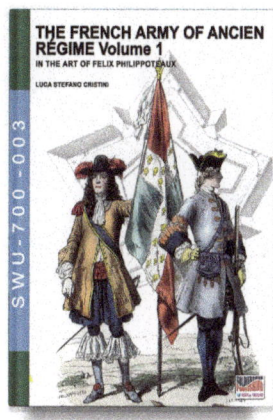

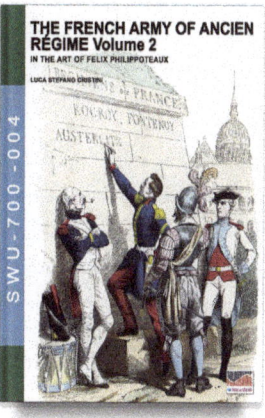

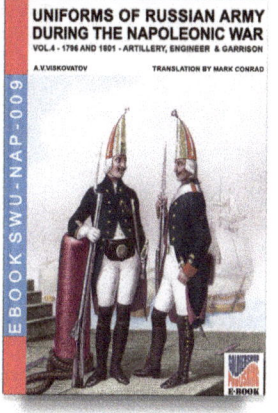

www.ingramcontent.com/pod-product-compliance
Lightning Source LLC
Chambersburg PA
CBHW051851140626
46547CB00034BA/3099